Written and illustrated by **ANNE-MARIE CONSTANT**

WASTE NOT WANT NOT

MINERALS

Burke Books **B** LONDON * TORONTO
* NEW YORK

All the things we use every day,
which we don't get from plants or animals,
we get from the earth.
Some of them are made from minerals—
things we take from the earth—
which may run out one day.

All the same . . .

we throw many things away.

From bottle caps
to satellites,
we use metals to make
an enormous number of the things we need
in modern life. And metals are minerals.

4

Let's look at a car
and see what minerals we use to make it:

iron

zinc

nickel

aluminium

lead (for the battery)

platinum (for the electrical equipment)

mercury (for the paint)

rubber and plastics (made from petrol)

To run it we need
petrol, diesel fuel or gas, and motor oils
—all made from crude oil.
We drive on roads made of bitumen or concrete.

We use a great many minerals
to make and run cars, lorries and trains,
so if we are wise we won't waste them.

diamond

sapphire

turquoise

jade figure
from Mexico

necklace in gold
and cornelian
from ancient Rome

Some minerals are particularly valuable
because they are rare and have special properties.
Gold, silver, platinum and precious,
semi-precious and other fine stones
become even more valuable
when they are used in works of art.
When we look at these objects
we can imagine all the ages
through which they have passed,
without changing.

alabaster statue from
ancient Egypt

Not all stones are "precious".
But they all have their uses and beauty.
Stone, marble and granite have been used
throughout history to build outstanding monuments.

antique sculpture
from Africa

Sculptors also use minerals
to express their art.
Potters, glassblowers
and other craftsmen make use of
earth, clay and sand.

Italian sculpture
from the Middle Ages

amphora, or
ancient vase

Indian pottery

These minerals are still used,
with other, more modern materials, in building.
Although they are getting more and more expensive
they are more and more in demand,
because there are more and more people on earth
and they all need shelter and somewhere to work.
We can see that it is becoming more necessary
than ever before to recover these valuable materials,
when buildings are knocked down,
and to use them over again.

concrete

slate

zinc

glass

iron

brick

stone

gravel

The best thing would be to make sure
that these fine materials,
provided by nature,
are used to make the world
more beautiful.
Unfortunately
this doesn't always happen.
Pollution makes buildings ugly
and eats away the stone of artistic monuments.
Sometimes it might be better for everyone
if old buildings were restored
instead of being knocked down.
This would be a good idea
from the human point of view,
as well as preventing waste.

A lot of modern materials
are made from coal and crude oil.
For instance: plastics

                  artificial fabrics

                  synthetic knitwear

                  detergents

                  paints, etc. . . .

If we waste all these things
we are wasting nature's own products.

An American study worked out that
the ordinary citizen throws away,
in his lifetime:
    10,000 bottles
    17,500 tins
    more than two cars
    35 tyres
    126 tonnes of rubbish . . .

Twenty tonnes of raw materials are mined
and processed per person per year (in America).
Since the number of people on earth
is increasing, this situation cannot go on.

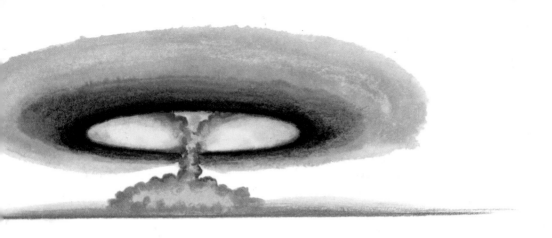

Uranium, plutonium, thorium . . .
these are metals which can release atomic energy.
By using radioactive substances
for nuclear experiments,
and even for the production of energy,
man is putting the whole earth in danger.

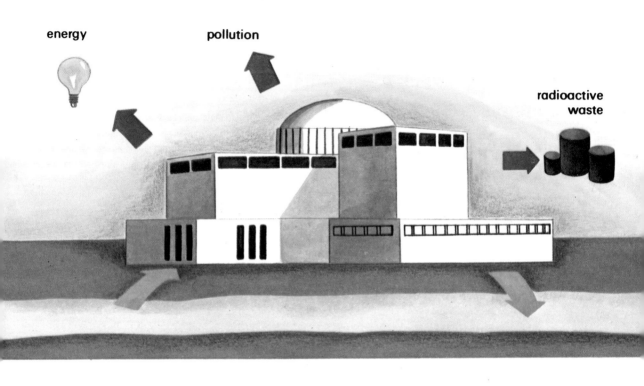

energy

pollution

radioactive
waste

In fact, radioactive fallout and waste
cause pollution of the air, water and earth.
This affects all living things,
quite apart from the danger of atomic war!

21

As you can see, by giving us her minerals
nature is making us a priceless gift.
But unfortunately in many cases
she is poorly rewarded.
In fact, by tearing her riches out of the earth,
man is wounding and damaging nature.

The processing industries pollute air,
earth and water.
By careless use of them,
man changes natural materials
into evil forces which cannot be controlled.

These materials are getting rarer
at an increasing speed.
What can we do to save them?

Use them only with good reason.
Recover used materials and used metals.

Recycled materials can be re-used.
For example, new glass can be made from
crushed, used glass

> saving sand
> saving soda
> saving energy.

Waste materials can be used as fuel
to heat houses and run factories (saving energy).
There is a factory near Rome
which sorts household rubbish and runs
by burning the waste which cannot be re-used.
It would also be a good idea
to make stronger cars and other machines
so that they wouldn't need to be replaced so often.

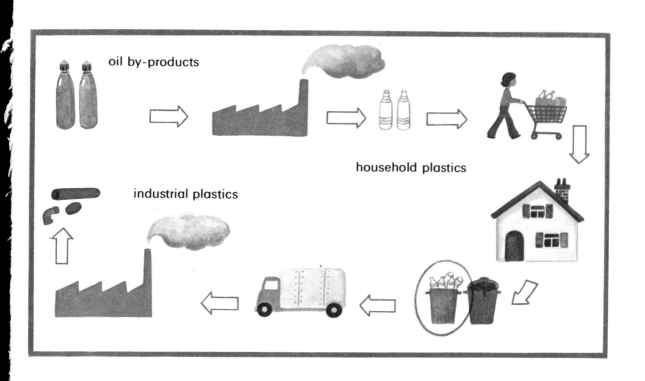

oil by-products

household plastics

industrial plastics

Industrial plastics can also be made from used plastics.

There are great hopes now
of finding new sources of raw materials
at the bottom of the sea; nodules, for example:
Nodules are metal crusts which collect
round a hard core (such as a shark's tooth).
The metal crusts consist of: cobalt
                                iron
                                manganese
                                copper
                                nickel
                                titanium.
New stocks of these minerals
have been discovered underwater
which are one hundred times greater
than the stocks found on land.

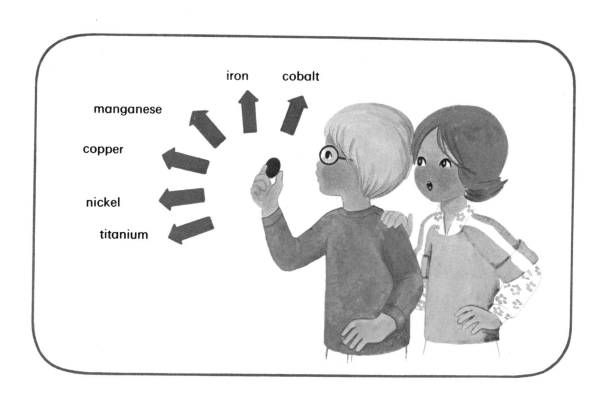

But the nodules lie at great depths
and it is important when collecting them
not to harm animal and plant life under
the sea, or cause pollution.

Let's take care of buildings,
whether they are old or new.

Take care of ordinary, everyday things,
even your toys.

Look after materials
so that they don't get spoiled.
Don't help to rob nature
by buying things and throwing them away
right and left.

Help to collect special types of rubbish.

Save energy.

Things to think about

1 Do you think that all the materials
   taken from the earth
   are always used in the most practical way?
   Find some examples of waste.

2 Find out what goes into the making of:

                              a brick
                              a tile
                              concrete
                              cement
                              glass
                              cast iron

3 What would happen if human beings
   used up all the minerals in the world?

ISBN 0 222 00524 6 SOFTBACK

ISBN 0 222 00516 5 HARDBOUND

BURKE PUBLISHING COMPANY LIMITED
PEGASUS HOUSE, 116-120 GOLDEN LANE, LONDON EC1Y 0TL, ENGLAND
BURKE PUBLISHING (CANADA) LIMITED
TORONTO, ONTARIO, CANADA
BURKE PUBLISHING COMPANY INC.
540 BARNUM AVENUE, BRIDGEPORT, CONNECTICUT 06608, USA
PRINTED IN GREAT BRITAIN BY
UNWIN BROTHERS LIMITED, GRESHAM PRESS, OLD WOKING, SURREY